THE
POWER
OF
WORSHIP

31 Days of Drawing Closer to God
In Worship

DR. MAKISHA DAVIS

Printed in the United States of America
ISBN: 978-1-965441-09-1

CONTENTS

ACKNOWLEDGEMENT

All praise, honor, and glory to the Holy Spirit for guiding me in the writing of this book. I am grateful for the support team that has been placed around me to encourage me throughout this assignment. I thank my husband, Bishop Kendall Davis; my family; Crossing Ministries; Bishop James Ross and United Christian Communion; Bishop Murvel Williams and Cover the Children Ministries; Pastor Carolyn Cole and By Faith Ministries; and Pastor Wakishia Lacour and Faith, Prayer, and Deliverance Ministry for their support. Thank you, Lord.

PREFACE

This book is designed to encourage believers to embrace a lifestyle of worship to God that will lead them to continually fall in love with Him. It is my prayer that you, the readers, will discover how worship will improve your everyday lives and strengthen your relationship with the Lord through spiritual insight and profound experiences. Each day inspires reflection and action, guiding you to express your devotion and love to God. *For an enjoyable experience while reading this book, after you have engaged with the daily content, take a moment to read the chapter of the daily scripture in the Bible. Use the worship reflection to note any additional praises that resonate with you from the chapter. Spend a few moments reflecting on your reading, then transition to the glory moment setting to capture what flows from your heart. Finally, wrap up your day's experience by scanning the QR code that will guide you into a moment of worship.* It is my hope that you meet God in new ways through this 31-day interaction. Walk with the Holy Spirit as He leads you into a deeper encounter with God. May God bless you richly.

SURRENDER

Psalm 46:10
He says, "Be still, and know that I am
God; I will be exalted among the nations,
I will be exalted in the earth."

Having a spirit of surrender is essential when coming before God in worship. Surrender, within a biblical framework, denotes the act of yielding or submitting to God's authority and will. It requires letting go of personal control and putting trust in God's power and plan. It reveals not only the humble nature of our hearts but also reflects a profound faith in witnessing God's presence among us. As we embrace humility, we often discover ourselves more open to the guidance and inspiration of God. This openness leads to life encounters that make us victorious. His presence brings a sense of peace and comfort to the innermost part of our existence.

In the middle of life's rough terrain, this Psalm tells us, there is a place of stillness set aside for each of us. In a moment of worship, there is a stillness that comes from being in God's presence. This stillness provides us strength as we continue to serve God with all our being. Stillness also elevates us to God's insight; one of the reasons for exaltation is to be in the place God has deemed so that we may grasp life's circumstances from a spiritual view, also being intentional about bringing God glory. This level of worship opens our ears to hear God and our eyes to see and experience His love in our lives. This profound experience invites us to embrace our vulnerabilities and nurture a stronger bond with God. In this act of surrendering in worship, we discover strength and clarity, leading us to our true calling and assisting us in navigating the complexities of our journey. **Let us worship God!**

WORSHIP REFLECTION

_____
_____
_____
_____
_____
_____
_____
_____
_____
_____
_____

WORSHIP ENCOUNTERS

_____
_____
_____
_____
_____
_____
_____
_____
_____
_____

Agnus Dei

REPENTANCE

---

2 Chronicles 7:14

If my people, who are called by my name,
will humble themselves and pray and seek
my face and turn from their wicked ways,
then I will hear from heaven, and I will
forgive their sin and will heal their land.

An established worship life with God teaches us that approaching Him requires clean hands and a pure heart (Psalm 24:4-6). Such obedience is essential because He is a holy God, whose essence is entirely pure and whose holiness is distinct from what is ordinary to humanity. He expects His children to embody the same qualities as His word states, that we are to be holy as He is holy (Leviticus 21:8, Exodus 19:6, 1 Peter 1:16). The Bible emphasizes this point three times, highlighting that our worship lifestyle of holiness mirrors His presence in our lives. Embracing obedience to God emerges as a fundamental pathway to achieving true holiness, reflecting the pure essence of a God whose holiness stands apart from any human understanding. This spiritual quality is not merely an abstract concept but a tangible standard for children of God, who are called to embody these virtues in their daily lives. As the Bible indicates the importance of holiness, it emphasizes that living a lifestyle rooted in worship and reverence towards God is essential.

When we sin, it is an offense against God's authority and holiness, and it hinders our worship. God provided a way for us through repentance to engage in the relationship He envisioned for all His children. Today's verses reveal that God has established a specific process for repentance. The biblical meaning of repentance is "Metanoeó," which signifies to think differently or to reconsider afterwards. God desired for His children to abandon their sinful paths and seek Him instead. The initial step in this process is that God requires His children to uphold a humble attitude; pride and humility cannot coexist. The next step involves praying and seeking His presence; this act of worship helps us to refocus on God's will in our lives. The last step involves separating oneself from those things (sins) that go against the will of God and the essence of His holiness. By making these intentional choices, it causes us to cultivate our worship and draws us closer to God as our life reflects His glory. **Let us worship God!**

WORSHIP REFLECTION

_____
_____
_____
_____
_____
_____
_____
_____
_____
_____
_____

WORSHIP ENCOUNTERS

_____
_____
_____
_____
_____
_____
_____
_____
_____
_____
_____

Nothing Else

TRUST IN GOD

Proverbs 3:5-6
*Trust in the Lord with all your heart and lean not
on your own understanding; in all your ways submit
to him, and he will make your paths straight.*

In worship to God, it is important to cultivate an intimate and trustworthy relationship to fully experience the manifestation of worship. As believers, we must first recognize that worshiping God is a way of life. This lifestyle requires commitment and sincerity, as it weaves together the threads of prayer, study, and service into a tapestry of devotion. Each act of worship serves to enhance our bond with God, fostering an intimacy that invites life-changing experiences into our lives. By remaining open to God's presence, we enrich our spiritual journey and unlock the potential for transformative effects that resonate far beyond ourselves. Offering God our entire heart in worship allows us to live fully in alignment with our faith, ultimately bringing us nearer to the heart of God.

Proverbs 3:5-6 teaches us the importance of placing our trust in God. The term "trust" translates to the Hebrew word "Batach," signifying a sense of confidence or reliance. By doing this, we relinquish all our understanding of the situation and anticipate God's movement as we adhere to His guidance. Having confidence is essential as we worship God. This worship is a deep-seated trust, which is not merely a passive state but an active engagement that enriches our worship, allowing us to acknowledge God's sovereignty and faithfulness. As we cultivate this reliance, we open ourselves to experiencing profound peace and direction among life's uncertainties. Ultimately, understanding and embodying "Batach" enhances our spiritual journey and transforms our daily experiences into the spiritual purpose and assurance of God. **Let us worship!**

WORSHIP REFLECTION

_____
_____
_____
_____
_____
_____
_____
_____
_____
_____
_____

WORSHIP ENCOUNTERS

_____
_____
_____
_____
_____
_____
_____
_____
_____
_____
_____

Trust In God

TRUE WORSHIP

John 4:23-24

*Yet a time is coming and has now come when
the true worshipers will worship the Father in
the Spirit and in truth, for they are the kind of
worshipers the Father seeks. God is spirit, and his
worshipers must worship in the Spirit and in truth.*

Living a lifestyle of worship requires us to approach God with sincerity, and we come to understand our truth through the relationship we cultivate with Him. This relationship begins with us exploring and nurturing our spiritual development. Just as a newborn baby enters the world without understanding or knowing who they are and who they are called to be, the baby clings to the familiar heartbeat and grows and develops as they discover their life purpose. Similarly, as we embark on our spiritual journey, we hold onto the heartbeat of God that brings us nearer to Him, revealing our identity and purpose. In this moment, we can present our worship to God. By understanding who He is, we gain the opportunity to uncover our true selves. Embracing a spiritual journey in worship to God is akin to the profound growth of a child discovering their place in the world, where each step taken brings us closer to understanding our true identity and purpose. As we navigate this path, we learn to attune ourselves to God's heartbeat, allowing His presence to guide us and illuminate our lives. Through heartfelt worship, we peel away the layers of societal expectations and self-doubt, revealing the authentic selves that God created us to be.

In John chapter 4, the Bible does not provide a name for the Samaritan woman; her identity is defined by her ethnicity and circumstances until her transformative encounter with Christ Jesus. The conversation between the two allows this woman to discover the heartbeat of God, enabling her to grow and develop spiritually, discover her identity, and fulfill the purpose for which she was created—ultimately bringing glory to God. Let us examine this verse from John 4:23-24 more closely. In these passages of scripture, we observe that the Father is in search of "True," represented by the Greek term "Aléthinos," which signifies sincerity. Additionally, the term "Worshippers" is accompanied by the Greek word "Proskuneó," which signifies bowing down in a gesture of adoration. This encounter with Christ afforded the woman the opportunity to acquire insight that would help her establish a proper spiritual relationship with God. This relationship provided her with an internal understanding and altered her perspective on her external circumstances. True worship leads us to surrender everything we have known, transforming us into all that God desires and created us to be. Let us step forward today to offer God our genuine worship. **Let us worship!**

WORSHIP REFLECTION

_____
_____
_____
_____
_____
_____
_____
_____
_____
_____
_____

WORSHIP ENCOUNTERS

_____
_____
_____
_____
_____
_____
_____
_____
_____
_____
_____

Alpha and Omega

LORD YOU ARE GOOD

Psalm 100:5
For the Lord is good and his love endures forever;
his faithfulness continues through all generations.

Our worship reflects the goodness of the Lord, and there we experience God's love. By participating in worship practices, we come to appreciate His unchanging love. Every act of worship, whether it's through song, prayer, words, or coming together as a community, beautifully reminds us of the grace God shows through His love. As we explore worship in faith, we not only celebrate His attributes but also nurture our relationship with God. Giving God our worship transforms into a wonderful journey that celebrates God's love and enhances the lives of everyone involved.

The journey of understanding God's love through worship reveals a profound interplay between personal spirituality and communal faith. As we participate in worship, we often discover transformative impacts in our daily lives. The importance of community in worship cannot be stressed; it provides an essential foundation for faith and belonging, allowing Christians to share their experiences and grow. It provides hope to others and motivates them to grow closer to God. This produces witnesses of God's kindness. This reinforces the belief that worship is not just an act, but a means to greater affection for God. These daily expressions, based on biblical teachings, demonstrate the core of God's love, encouraging us to consider how worship might benefit both personal and collective spiritual journeys. **Let us worship God!**

WORSHIP REFLECTION

_____
_____
_____
_____
_____
_____
_____
_____
_____
_____
_____

GLORY MOMENTS

_____
_____
_____
_____
_____
_____
_____
_____
_____
_____
_____

Lord You are Good

MORE THAN ENOUGH

Ephesians 3:20-21
Now to Him who is able to do exceedingly
abundantly above all that we ask or think,
according to the power that works in us, to
Him be glory in the church by Christ Jesus to
all generations, forever and ever. Amen

As believers, we serve a God who is abundantly sufficient. In the book of Genesis, we observe that everything was in order before man was created, as He is the God of abundance. In times of distress, we may find ourselves concentrating on our problems and overlooking the provisions that God has made for us, which can lead us to withdraw in our worship. However, God provides us with His assurance through His word. God reassures us of His unwavering presence and promises, encouraging us to shift our focus from our troubles to His goodness. The exploration of God's abundant sufficiency in worship reveals a profound truth: believers are called to recognize and celebrate the richness of God's provisions, as illustrated in the creation narrative of Genesis. God reassures us of His love and the plans He has for us, encouraging us to worship beyond our circumstances. By embracing this perspective, worship transforms into an expression of gratitude for God's perpetual abundance, which strengthens our faith.

Today's scripture highlights the advantages of our worship to our Lord and Savior, Jesus Christ. Our worship relationship grants us entry into the kingdom of God. There are times in our lives when we make our prayer requests known to God, and the magnitude of who He is in our lives transcends what our current circumstances may be telling us. Ephesians reminds us that God is capable of exceeding our thoughts and imaginations. The passage also says He meets our current and future needs. It is essential for us to maintain a worship relationship, allowing the power of God to be revealed and ensuring that He receives the glory from our lives. The manifestation of His glory and the fullness of His strength in our lives leads us to triumph. **Let us worship!**

WORSHIP REFLECTION

_____
_____
_____
_____
_____
_____
_____
_____
_____
_____

GLORY MOMENTS

_____
_____
_____
_____
_____
_____
_____
_____
_____
_____

Jireh

REFINER

Zechariah 13:9

I will put into the fire; I will refine them like silver and test them like gold. They will call on my name and I will answer them; I will say, 'They are my people, and they will say, 'The Lord is our God.'

Pursuing a lifestyle of worship leads us through a process of refinement, eliminating the impurities from our lives, allowing us to present God with pure worship. This act is significant as it reflects the holy nature of God. To experience the holiness of God, we must first embody holiness ourselves. The process of refinement is essential, even if it can be challenging. As one navigates the challenges of refinement, we find that each trial strengthens our faith and enriches our worship to God. The journey of refinement through faith reveals the profound depths of Jesus Christ's sacrifice, which secures believers' righteous standing before God. Being refined can be uncomfortable for the flesh, yet it reveals the beauty of the spirit that provides genuine worship to God. This discomfort often leads to personal growth and a more profound understanding of our faith. Overall, it's truly through this transformation that believers can authentically connect with and honor God. Our worship brings us closer to God, which in turn heightens our awareness of Him in our everyday lives.

Worship to God presents a level of intimacy that allows us to become pliable in His hand. God's hand is used to shape, build, and strengthen us as we prepare to move forward in the purpose for which we were created with purity. Because of the spiritual nourishment we receive from this relationship, we are able to confidently accept who we really are and follow our purpose in life. Giving ourselves over to God's will transforms us into carriers of His love, which we then share with others who are greatly in need of His light. Zechariah highlights that there's a fire that refines believers to call on God's name, and what really encourages me is that each fire refines us in its own unique way. Some people might face health challenges and find themselves reaching out to Jehovah Rapha, our healer. Some people might find themselves in tough situations and need to reach out to Jehovah Jireh, our Provider. Some people find themselves in calamity and reach out to Jehovah Shalom, our peace.

His word says that when we call out, He will be there to answer us because we are His. This is precisely why we come together to offer our worship. **Let us Worship!**

WORSHIP REFLECTION

_____
_____
_____
_____
_____
_____
_____
_____
_____
_____
_____

GLORY MOMENTS

_____
_____
_____
_____
_____
_____
_____
_____
_____
_____
_____

Refiner

8

SANCTIFIED SPACES

Exodus 3:4-5

*When the Lord saw that he had gone over to look,
God called to him from within the bush, "Moses!
Moses!" And Moses said, "Here I am." "Do not come
any closer," God said. "Take off your sandals, for
the place where you are standing is holy ground."*

It is imperative that every believer have a sacred space where they meet with God. In this space, we engage in genuine worship, free from the distractions of life's concerns. It is at this point that we stand before God naked and unashamed; this stance represents the unveiling of our hearts before Him. This deep concentration on God enables us to perceive and listen to Him in the spirit. It is where we receive comfort and instructions for our lives and the lives of those around us. Through this connection, we are transformed, gaining clarity and purpose. As we embrace this sacred communion, our faith is strengthened.

On this level of worship, God reveals His desire to us. How often have we approached worship with the intention of seeking God's desire rather than our interests? Creating a sacred space to connect with God encourages us to approach with clean hands and a pure heart (Psalm 24:3-4). This reinforces the idea that true worship transcends mere ritual; it is an invitation to foster a genuine relationship with God as we navigate these spiritual paths together.

In Exodus, we discover that Moses encountered God through a burning bush, demonstrating that sacred spaces can manifest in unexpected ways. This encounter highlights the notion that divine revelations may manifest in surprising ways and places. It encourages us to contemplate the importance of embracing the extraordinary in our daily experiences. It is within the sacred spaces that we received guidance from God. Just as God disclosed to Moses that the ground beneath him was sacred. God gave Moses the Ten Commandments and instructions for the children of Israel on Mount Sinai in Exodus 20. In the sacred spaces, our ears become attuned to God's voice, and our understanding is illuminated to discern the perfect will of God for our lives. This highlights the advantage of having engaged in worship within sacred environments. **Let us worship!**

WORSHIP REFLECTION

_____
_____
_____
_____
_____
_____
_____
_____
_____
_____
_____
_____

GLORY MOMENTS

_____
_____
_____
_____
_____
_____
_____
_____
_____
_____
_____
_____

Bow Down

GLORY REVEALED

In the year that King Uzziah died, I saw the Lord, high and exalted, seated on a throne; and the train of his robe filled the temple. ² Above him were seraphim, each with six wings: With two wings they covered their faces, with two they covered their feet, and with two they were flying. ³ And they were calling to one another: "Holy, holy, holy is the Lord Almighty; the whole earth is full of his glory."

Have you ever taken a moment to contemplate the splendor of God and His incredible glory? The profound encounter described in Isaiah 6:1-3 illustrates the transformative power of God's magnificence in our lives. When we invite His presence, we experience a revelation of His glory, which is rooted in the Hebrew concept of "Kābôd," signifying not only His weightiness but also His immeasurable worth. This divine encounter reshapes our surroundings, infusing them with purpose and meaning as we become more attuned to the holiness that permeates our existence. Ultimately, acknowledging and embracing God's glory compels us to live with an increased consciousness of His presence, urging us to worship Him in our daily lives. The presence of God alone brings forth a revealed glory that changes the environment.

Communion with God in worship brings a splendor that shifts your focus away from your current situations and reveals who He is within those circumstances. The revelation serves as a gateway to the spiritual realm, enabling us to deepen our relationship with God and clarify our life's purpose. We see in Isaiah the revelation of how the angels understood their position of humility during worship in the presence of God. This awareness motivates us to embrace a humble and respectful attitude, realizing that authentic worship provides access to divine wisdom and transformation. Through encountering God's revealed presence in worship, we develop our ability to see and recognize God's voice and allow Him to lead us and provide us the ability to live intentionally in His love. **Let us worship!**

WORSHIP REFLECTION

_____
_____
_____
_____
_____
_____
_____
_____
_____
_____
_____

GLORY MOMENTS

_____
_____
_____
_____
_____
_____
_____
_____
_____
_____
_____

This is Glory

NO LIMITS

Act 16:25-26

About midnight Paul and Silas were praying and singing hymns to God, and the other prisoners were listening to them.[26] Suddenly there was such a violent earthquake that the foundations of the prison were shaken. At once all the prison doors flew open, and everyone's chains came loose.

Throughout our life journey, we may encounter instances where different circumstances hinder our ability to worship God. This serves as a clear sign that we have reached a point of being overwhelmed, reflecting the challenges we are facing in our worship. It is essential to assess what I refer to as the worship barometer; joy is often one of the first things to fade, leading us to feel frustrated and negative about even the smallest aspects of our surroundings. The second thing we do is adopt a casual approach to our commitment to God. Additionally, we often perceive prayer as a task. These are all indications that we have constrained our worship. The good news is that God is accessible and has not restricted our worship, so we don't have to stay in this state. We have the ability to worship at any moment and in any environment, as we were designed to worship God.

Paul and Silas demonstrated remarkable worship, as the confines of prison could not hinder the spirit within them. Their praise flowed freely, unrestrained by any limitations. They were not only liberated, but everyone present experienced liberation too. God would not permit anything to obstruct the praise or worship offered to Him by His children. Furthermore, worship always creates a transformative impact. Worship has the power to be an effective agent of transformation during times of despair, inspiring hope and rebirth even in the most dire situations. It serves as a reminder that faith can surpass physical limitations, uplifting spirits, and motivating those around us to increase their worship relationship with God. **Let us worship!**

WORSHIP REFLECTION

_____
_____
_____
_____
_____
_____
_____
_____
_____
_____

GLORY MOMENTS

_____
_____
_____
_____
_____
_____
_____
_____
_____
_____

No Limits

WHOLE HEART

Colossians 3:23-24
*Whatever you do, work at it with all your
heart, as working for the Lord, not for human
masters, ²⁴ since you know that you will receive
an inheritance from the Lord as a reward.
It is the Lord Christ you are serving.*

Devoting your entire heart to God provides a true
act of worship to Him. The term "worship" in this
context is derived from the Greek word "latreuó,"
which signifies the act of rendering service and devotion to God. This was depicted as priests attended to
the articles of God in the temple, fostering an atmosphere of worship. In our present time, we serve the
Lord Jesus Christ, and regardless of our position on
this life journey, it is our duty to offer worship through
our work. When we are at work, our hearts should be
filled with the opportunity to worship God. I recall
the monk known as Brother Lawrence, who in the

book "The Practice of the Presence of God" exemplified wholehearted service, stating, "What I do, I do unto God." His lifestyle was simple but significant, as he committed all he did to the Lord.

Ultimately, Paul's admonishment to the Colossians stands as a significant reminder of the essence of service grounded in Christ. By emphasizing the importance of Christ's role, he encourages believers to engage in their acts of worship and service wholeheartedly, nurturing a genuine relationship with God. Having gratitude and humility turns service into a joyous manifestation of faith. Paul also encourages people to have lasting worship experiences, which push them to develop a closer relationship with their spiritual practices and ensure that their commitment lasts continually. By employing this holistic method, Paul not only enhances the perception of service but also motivates a way of living that embodies genuine worship that lasts a lifetime. **Let us worship!**

WORSHIP REFLECTION

_____
_____
_____
_____
_____
_____
_____
_____
_____
_____
_____

GLORY MOMENTS

_____
_____
_____
_____
_____
_____
_____
_____
_____
_____
_____

"Your Majesty"

HOLY FOREVER

Hebrews 12:14

*Make every effort to live in peace with everyone and
to be holy; without holiness no one will see the Lord.*

Understanding holiness is essential for developing a
lifestyle of worship. Holiness is a quality that God
expects us to reflect as His beloved children. Hebrews
12:14 tells us that without holiness, no one will see
God. This verse uses the term holiness to describe
someone who is sanctified in both heart and life. In the
book titled "Spiritual Authority" by Watchman Nee, it
is noted that humanity's sin is a transgression against
God's authority or His holiness. Today, we believe
that the blood of Jesus Christ on the cross served as
the "price paid" for sin. His blood brings purification
to all who enter a relationship with Him, guiding us to
live our lives in accordance with the pattern He set for
us. We achieve this by following the guidance of the
Holy Spirit and embracing a life of holiness.

God always intended for us to experience life with Him both here on earth and in the heavens. Walking in holiness allows us to perceive life from a spiritual viewpoint, enabling us to see life through the lens of God's eyes. This prompts us to remain vigilant against distractions that may lead us astray, ensuring that we live our lives in a way that brings glory to God. I often declare, "God gets the glory, and we get the blessing." Walking in Holiness enables us to attain a peace that transcends the obstacles causing distress in our lives, maintaining our right standing with God. As we embrace this understanding as believers, we yearn to experience and dwell with Him in holiness for eternity. **Let us worship!**

WORSHIP REFLECTION

_____
_____
_____
_____
_____
_____
_____
_____
_____
_____
_____

GLORY MOMENTS

_____
_____
_____
_____
_____
_____
_____
_____
_____
_____
_____

Holy Forever

GOD'S PRESENCE

Psalm 16:11

*You make known to me the path of life; you
will fill me with joy in your presence, with
eternal pleasures at your right hand.*

Those who are in an intimate worship relationship
with God, experience the richness of spiritual ben-
efits of being in His presence in several ways. The
presence of God provides us with a level of peace that
is found in the center of our despair, yet at the same
time gives us understanding and guidance of His perfect will, which strengthens our faith. It is amazing to
know that we are not alone, and we have the one who
is the greatest in this universe and beyond standing
with and for us as stated in Romans 8:31. The deeper
our intimacy in worship to God, the greater our longing for His presence becomes. In Exodus 33:18, we
observe Moses pleading with God to see His Glory.
Once we have established a level of intimacy through

worship, the presence of God becomes something we crave endlessly. This worship takes us deeper into our spiritual relationship with God, causing us to gain an insightful perspective on life.

In Psalm 16:11, we observe that David developed a deep yearning for the presence of God. He understood that God provides clarity in life, accompanied by the joy of His presence. This also brings pleasure that transcends our natural environment and continues indefinitely. David understood that the presence of God brought favor, honor, and authority, which were essential as he guided a nation of people. When we fully commit ourselves to worshiping God, it fosters a relationship that enriches our successes in everything He has designed for us to fulfill, while simultaneously reflecting His glory. This relationship not only empowers us to achieve our potential but also allows us to shine a light on God's greatness in our lives. By aligning ourselves with His purpose, we become vessels of His love and truth in the world. **Let us worship!**

WORSHIP REFLECTION

_____
_____
_____
_____
_____
_____
_____
_____
_____
_____

GLORY MOMENTS

_____
_____
_____
_____
_____
_____
_____
_____
_____
_____

Holy Spirit Welcome

THIRSTY

Psalm 42:1-2

As the deer pants for the water brooks, so pants my soul for You, O God. ² My soul thirsts for God, for the living God.

Living a lifestyle of worship unto God brings an abundance of fulfillment and refreshment in the spirit. When the spirit and soul are nourished, it positively impacts how we interact with others and navigate negative situations. Worshipping God allows our spirit and soul to flow abundantly. It is through our abundance that we offer encouragement, support, and guidance to those who are spiritually depleted. It is essential to maintain a connection with God and engage in worship, allowing His presence to flow through us for the benefit of others as well as ourselves. When we stop responding in this way, we enter a state of drought and an intense longing for the fulfillment of God. This drought reflects a spiritual emptiness that arises when we neglect our worship relationship with God and cease to share our blessings.

The Palmist in 42:1-2 begins with a metaphor of the deer longing for a water brook. Recognizing that deer require water for their survival is crucial, as it influences their bodily functions, including digestion and blood circulation, and plays a role in the development of their antlers. The Hebrew word "pant" refers to a deep longing accompanied by a desperate craving. This imagery highlights the intensity of the psalmist's yearning for spiritual sustenance, akin to a deer's urgent need for water. It underscores the profound connection between physical needs and spiritual desires, illustrating the depth of longing for God's presence. This comparison emphasizes that just as a deer instinctively seeks water to survive, the psalmist expresses an essential desire for a relationship with God, suggesting that spiritual fulfillment is as vital as physical sustenance and is manifested through worship. Such imagery enriches our understanding of the human experience, intertwining the physical and spiritual realms. **Let us worship!**

WORSHIP REFLECTION

_____
_____
_____
_____
_____
_____
_____
_____
_____
_____
_____

GLORY MOMENTS

_____
_____
_____
_____
_____
_____
_____
_____
_____
_____

Thirsty

ALTAR

Genesis 8:20

*Noah constructed an altar to the LORD
and offered burnt offerings using some of
all the clean animals and clean birds.*

The altar is recognized as a holy space, serving as God's table where sacrifices and offerings are presented in worship. The altar serves as a sacred space where humanity engages in divine connection with God through worship. The term altar in Hebrew signifies "a location for slaughter and sacrifice." The first mention of an altar is found in the Old Testament, specifically in Genesis 8:20, where Noah constructed an altar to the LORD and offered burnt offerings using some of all the clean animals and clean birds. It was God who initiated the first sacrifice after sin entered the world, as described in Genesis 3, when Adam and Eve donned garments made of fig leaves. God provided them with more appropriate garments, sacrificing an animal to create the clothing. This act not only signifies the seriousness of sin but also foreshadows the ultimate sacrifice that would come later in biblical history. The altar, therefore, serves as a powerful symbol of worship, repentance, and the covenant relationship between God and humanity.

Today, the altar is known as a place for surrendering to God, which is vital to the worship lifestyle. Romans 12:1 states, "Therefore, I urge you, brothers and sisters, in view of God's mercy, to offer your bodies as a living sacrifice, holy and pleasing to God—this is your true and proper worship." Paul perceives sacrifice as a continuous, vibrant act of worship, setting it apart from the lifeless sacrifices of the Old Covenant. This entails committing oneself wholly to God, embodying a life characterized by holiness and service. This commitment invites us to reflect on our daily actions and choices, aligning them with God's will. By doing so, they not only honor their faith but also inspire others to engage in a similar journey of devotion and worship. **Let us worship!**

WORSHIP REFLECTION

_____
_____
_____
_____
_____
_____
_____
_____
_____
_____
_____

GLORY MOMENTS

_____
_____
_____
_____
_____
_____
_____
_____
_____
_____
_____

This Altar

RELYING ON THE SPIRIT

John 14:26

But the Advocate, the Holy Spirit, whom the Father will send in my name, will teach you all things and will remind you of everything I have said to you.

Embracing a lifestyle of worship is crucial for us to fully understand what is revealed to us in the spiritual realm; we must seek the insight of the Holy Spirit. There is nothing more frustrating than encountering something that you cannot comprehend or identify. The emergence of sin has led to a blurring of our vision and a tarnishing of our capacity for complete understanding. The Holy Spirit understands the complete will of God and is aware of God's purpose for our lives. In John 14:26, Jesus tells the disciples that the Holy Spirit will be sent from the Father, and as the saying goes, "Father knows best." Indeed, our heavenly father understands precisely what we require and the timing that serves our best interests. The Holy

Spirit is fully aware of His role in our lives, yet some struggle to rely on Him. Finally realizing our need for the Holy Spirit and embracing His will, we become capable of seeing and comprehending the journey we are currently on. This understanding allows us to navigate our experiences with greater clarity and purpose. By accepting the guidance of the Holy Spirit, we can align ourselves more closely with God's intentions for our lives.

In the Gospel of John 14:26, the Holy Spirit is referred to as the Advocate. The Greek term for this is "paráklētos," which signifies a legal advocate who makes the right judgment. This is truly remarkable, as we frequently face challenges in making decisions. However, when we pray and trust in the Holy Spirit, our circumstances will continually align with God's intentions for us. The Holy Spirit possesses great wisdom. He is excellent not only in spiritual matters but also in guiding us on how to navigate worldly affairs. Entering worship with the insight and perspective of the Holy Spirit enriches the experience, instilling in us a desire to be guided by Him in every aspect of our daily lives. Indeed, the Holy Spirit is essential. Without His influence, we may struggle to find clarity and purpose. Embracing His guidance empowers us to make decisions through faith and draws us closer to the path that has been intended for us. **Let us worship!**

WORSHIP REFLECTION

_____
_____
_____
_____
_____
_____
_____
_____
_____

GLORY MOMENTS

_____
_____
_____
_____
_____
_____
_____
_____
_____

I Need Thee

OPEN DOOR

Psalm 95:6

*Come, let us bow down in worship, let us
kneel before the LORD our Maker!*

The psalmist reminds us that we are welcome to enter through the door and assume our place in worship. This invitation to worship encourages us to enter through the spiritual door and partake in a life-changing spiritual experience. The act of entering goes beyond the physical movement; it places worshippers in a realm of reverence and intimacy with God, enabling us to embrace our faith and spiritual identity fully. When approaching kings, it was customary practice to bow down as a sign of respect and homage. This was done in order to show respect and humility. The fact that you were kneeling was a sign that you were prepared to engage in conversation and that the king already had your attention. This psalmist, King David, had a great deal of experience with the etiquette because he had previously served kings before becoming one himself.

I cherish the fact that, although we serve the King of Kings and the Lord of Lords, it is His desire for us to approach Him prepared to offer worship. It requires us to give Him our undivided attention, which means He becomes our focus, and we are free from distractions and humbled in spirit. When we take this approach to offer our worship, it will not be rejected but received by God, inviting us to draw closer. The fragrance of worship releases a delightful atmosphere that gives us strength to bear under the weight of God's glory. **Let us worship!**

WORSHIP REFLECTION

_____
_____
_____
_____
_____
_____
_____
_____
_____
_____
_____
_____

GLORY MOMENTS

_____
_____
_____
_____
_____
_____
_____
_____
_____
_____
_____
_____

Wide As The Sky

BREATHE

Genesis 2:7
Then the LORD God formed a man from the dust of the ground and breathed into his nostrils the breath of life, and the man became a living being.

In Genesis 2:7, we find that the very existence of human life was founded on the breath of God and the hand of God. This verse reveals that God formed, and the term used in Hebrew for formed is "Aphar," which translates to earth or dust. This indicates that He took some of the earth in the form of dust to shape man, yet life had not been given. The passage highlights that although God physically formed man from the earth, it was through His breath, referred to as "Naphach" in Hebrew, meaning to blow into, that life was given, showing the divine connection between the Creator and creation. This points out the belief that human life is a precious gift from God, encompassing both physical and spiritual dimensions. Our worship to God allows us to continue to access the spiritual realm while living on the earth.

Worship is the portal that reveals God's presence in our lives, causing us to encounter the manifestation of His love. Worship is a love language that brings about the intimate relationship between God and believers. This relationship fosters the intertwining of our spirit with the Spirit of God that leads and guides us in our daily living. This causes us to walk in obedience to God through the instructions of His word, thus making us successful overcomers on the pathway of life. Therefore, worship is a lifestyle. **Let us worship!**

WORSHIP REFLECTION

_____
_____
_____
_____
_____
_____
_____
_____
_____
_____

GLORY MOMENTS

_____
_____
_____
_____
_____
_____
_____
_____
_____
_____

Breathe

DWELL

Psalm 140:13

Surely the righteous shall give thanks to Your
name; The upright shall dwell in Your presence.

As believers, it is important that our worship lifestyle remains even when we are in difficult situations. Our worship keeps us in the presence of God.
What we know about His presence is that is will show
us the way of life and that means in any state we
find ourselves in and in His presence is the fullness
of Joy, an inner satisfaction comes when we dwell in
His presence, also we are able to delight in His spiritual pleasure that bring about our purpose that brings
God glory (Psalm 16:11). We truly have to understand that we live this life because of Him and to Him.
This means we were created for Him (Isaiah 43:7)
God takes pleasure in our worship and obedience that
brings about a bond that is not easily disturbed when
we find ourselves going through the rough terrains

of life. Through our worship to God, we capture a peace that comes from the spiritual dwelling place.

In Psalm 140:13, the psalmist expresses gratitude, recognizing that despite his challenging circumstances, the assurance of living in God's presence brings comfort. This assurance strengthens our confidence and motivates others as they observe us navigating life's challenges. Dwelling with God leads us to increase our love for Him. This love builds our desire to seek to please Him as we live the life He has provided for us, and we become more equipped when facing hardship with hope and perseverance as we cultivate this relationship. Through hope, we increase our faith, causing us to stand victorious while offering heartfelt worship to our God. **Let us worship!**

WORSHIP REFLECTION

_____
_____
_____
_____
_____
_____
_____
_____
_____
_____
_____

GLORY MOMENTS

_____
_____
_____
_____
_____
_____
_____
_____
_____
_____
_____

Stay With Me

GET THE GLORY

Luke 4:8

*Jesus answered, "It is written: 'Worship the
Lord your God and serve him only.*

What I love about worship is that it draws in the
presence of God, filling the empty spaces in our
souls, which kindles a fire to live holy and a desire to
do His will. Many seek validation from many things,
but true validation comes from God. This validation shows up in worship, through which those who
surrender with their whole heart receive a powerful
exchange. Psalm 61:3 informs us that God gives the oil
of joy for those in sorrow and the garment of praise
for those in despair. When we depart from our intimate place of worship, we are covered with the Lord's
imputed righteousness, enabling us to live uprightly
before Him and others. Just as Moses returned from
the intimate place in the mountains to the children of
Israel, he was seen as one who had been in the pres-

ence of God. This is how others perceive us when we have worshiped with God. It also encourages others to approach God, thereby giving Him the glory

In Luke 4:8, Jesus makes a profound statement as He is in the thick of a spiritual battle with Satan. Although Jesus was tempted, he did not yield; instead, he responded by saying, Worship the Lord your God and serve him only. This statement exemplifies the strength and conviction that accompany a dedicated lifestyle of worship. It doesn't mean we seek difficulty; it signifies that we overcome through worship and the Word of God. In our victories, God receives the glory while we enjoy the blessings. Worship cultivates a mindset that emphasizes victory over defeat as we face challenges and struggles. This mindset shifts our perspective, allowing us to see challenges as opportunities for growth and while seeking God. Ultimately, it reinforces the idea that true worship empowers us to rise above adversity while honoring God. **Let us worship!**

WORSHIP REFLECTION

_____
_____
_____
_____
_____
_____
_____
_____
_____
_____
_____

GLORY MOMENTS

_____
_____
_____
_____
_____
_____
_____
_____
_____
_____
_____

Hallelujah

SET THE ATMOSPHERE

2 Kings 3:16

But now bring me a musician." Then it happened, when the musician played, that the hand of the LORD came upon him.

What is the posture of our heart when we approach God in worship? It is vital that it be cleaned and ready for offering worship from a pure space. This brings about an atmosphere that sends an aroma to the heavenlies, where the presence of God is released. We must understand that when we enter worship, there is a heart examination. Why? Because God sees the heart (1 Sam 16:7), and it is the heart that displays our true position. Many attempt to enter worship with God from the outward appearance and leave His presence without an encounter because the atmosphere was not set. We must understand that the Lord is the same yesterday, today, and forevermore (Heb 13:8), and His position does not change. So we have to ask ourselves why I am not experiencing the shift in the atmosphere that releases God's presence. The remedy to such an issue is checking our heart posture. The right heart posture is essential in worship because it determines the authenticity and depth of our connection with God. When our hearts are humble, pure, and genuinely seeking God, we create an environment where His presence can dwell and move freely. A sincere heart allows us to worship in spirit and truth, rather than out of routine or for outward appearances. This openness invites transformation and aligns our desires with God's will, ensuring that our worship is not just an action but an encounter that honors Him fully.

In 2 Kings 3:16, the king sought out musicians, understanding that their melodies would stir the heart and invite the presence of God, allowing him to hear divine guidance. How often have we taken part in worship without truly reflecting the spirit of worship in our hearts? Nonetheless, as the choir or praise team begins to sing, our hearts start to shift, and before we realize it, our mouths are open, hands are extended, and our emotions are released, yearning for God's presence. The change in atmosphere allowed individuals with the right heart posture to experience an encounter with God. God's sovereignty allows Him to enter the room and meet us exactly where we are, providing what is necessary to sustain our faith as we serve Him. **Let us worship!**

WORSHIP REFLECTION

_____
_____
_____
_____
_____
_____
_____
_____
_____
_____
_____

GLORY MOMENTS

_____
_____
_____
_____
_____
_____
_____
_____
_____
_____
_____

Atmosphere

MEDITATION MOMENT

Psalm 19:14
*May these words of my mouth and this
meditation of my heart be pleasing in your
sight, Lord, my Rock and my Redeemer.*

In worship, a profound richness unfolds as we enter the spiritual realm, where your concerns begin to fade, and the overwhelming peace of God surrounds you. This peaceful space places us in a position of stillness that encourages reflection on the goodness of God. Several believers find it challenging to reach a state of quietness, particularly in today's world, where daily life presents such rapid demands. The fast pace of life often leads believers to lose sight of significant spiritual opportunities with God. However, when we recognize the value of meditation in God's presence, and the amazing experience we live in. It becomes a place of reverence and worship to God, as well as a place where we desire to live daily. This demonstrates how important it is for us to create meditation time in order to commune with God. The practice helps believers grow their faith. Despite the distractions of life, once we include meditation as a part of our worship, it begins to enhance our spiritual insight for life success.

David clearly grasped this as he authored Psalm 19. Meditation opens our spirit to God, enabling Him to fill us and guide us in our daily living. This level of worship prepares us as we interact with others, offering encouragement and embracing difficult situations. Worship through meditation develops our spiritual awareness, causing us to become more discerning on this Christian journey. David understood the importance of his approach to God, desiring nothing more than to enter God's presence with a sweet aroma that would be pleasing to God. As we draw near to God in worship and meditate on His goodness and His role in our lives, it leads us to a powerful worship encounter with Him. **Let us worship!**

WORSHIP REFLECTION

_____
_____
_____
_____
_____
_____
_____
_____
_____
_____

GLORY MOMENTS

_____
_____
_____
_____
_____
_____
_____
_____
_____
_____

Great Are You Lord

HEART OF GRATITUDE

Ephesians 5:20

Always giving thanks to God the Father for everything, in the name of our Lord Jesus Christ.

Entering worship with a heart full of gratitude reveals our sincere attitude towards God. We recognize that God looks at the heart, as indicated in 1 Sam. 16:7, *"But the Lord said to Samuel, 'Do not consider his appearance or his height, for I have rejected him. The Lord does not look at the things people look at. People look at the outward appearance, but the Lord looks at the heart."* Entering the presence of God with a grateful heart signifies our readiness for a glorious encounter with the Lord. This encounter prepares us to become overcomers as we walk through life challenges. Having a heart of gratitude in worship unlocks doors of purpose that enrich our spirit, resulting in an appreciation that inspires us to express a greater love for God and His people. This opens an opportunity for those around us to consider their disposition and outlook on life, thus giving the hope needed for every situation that they may experience. This posture can become contagious, influencing our surroundings to prepare for a move of God.

This mindset helps us to put Ephesians 5:20 into practice. As we fully engage in our worship with a heart full of gratitude, the weight of negative situations diminishes in our eyes, allowing us to concentrate on the spiritual aspect of the issue. This shift brings forth a level of peace and thankfulness to God, as the resolution manifests and leads to a sense of closure. Through cultivating an attitude of gratitude in worship also allows us to strengthen our faith, which in turn encourages us to have faith in God's timing and guidance. Because of this transformation, not only does our worship experience become more meaningful, but it also really enhances how we worship and gives us the strength and hope to tackle life's challenges in a fresh way. **Let us worship!**

WORSHIP REFLECTION

_____
_____
_____
_____
_____
_____
_____
_____
_____
_____
_____

GLORY MOMENTS

_____
_____
_____
_____
_____
_____
_____
_____
_____
_____
_____

Thank you

WEIGHT OF YOUR GLORY

Exodus 34:34-35

Then the cloud covered the tent of meeting, and
the glory of the LORD filled the tabernacle.
³⁵Moses was not able to enter the tent of meeting
because the cloud had settled on it, and the
glory of the LORD filled the tabernacle.

When we enter worship and the glory of the Lord is present, it signifies His approval of the space we occupy, and our response should be governed by the spirit that is within us. The passage reveals that we have entered a transformed spiritual setting, necessitating a spiritual response. 1 Corinthians 1:29 informs us that "no flesh shall glory in His presence," because the flesh in its natural state is sinful. God communes with us by the Spirit and through His Spirit. Worship is vital to the righteous, as it invites God. Psalm 34:15 says that God sees the good people and hears their cries. Worship from the righteous children of God

presents a sound that God hears and draws in His
glory.

The weight of God's glory implies that He has filled
the space. As we see in Exodus 34, God's glory filled
the tabernacle. The word "glory" signifies the weight
in a positive sense of the splendor of God. We see
that God's glory rested on the tabernacle. There are
times in our lives when we see the move of God,
and we must take the position to sit and wait for the
instruction of the Lord; this is a part of worship to
God. It displays a level of respect for God and the
holy things that He set apart. The weight of God's
glory implies that He is in our midst. In today's time,
many enter the secret spaces God has set up for us and
are unaware of his presence. Jacob says in Genesis
28:16, "God was in the place, and I did not know."
Worship allows us to sense the presence of God and
heed His move. The result is what was seen in Exodus
34: when God's glory was resting on the tabernacle
by the cloud, the children of Israel would not pack
up and move. For they waited until God's weighted
glory lifted. In our lives, we must do the same. Once
we enter worship and the glory of God is present,
we must respond as led by the Spirit in honor and
respect to God. This means that, just as the Israelites
waited for God's glory to guide their movements, we
too should be attentive to the Spirit's leading during

worship. By doing so, we show reverence for God's presence and align our actions with His divine will. **Let us worship!**

WORSHIP REFLECTION

_____
_____
_____
_____
_____
_____
_____
_____
_____
_____
_____

GLORY MOMENTS

_____
_____
_____
_____
_____
_____
_____
_____
_____
_____
_____

Let Your Glory Fall

FILLING THE WELL

Psalm 81:10

*I am the Lord your God, who brought
you up out of Egypt.
Open wide your mouth and I will fill it.*

What I find remarkable is that when we engage God in worship, He fills the voids within our souls. Surrendering in worship leads us to the fullness of God. In life, we encounter numerous challenges that can drain us and cause our souls to feel distressed. However, we express our gratitude for God's love and kindness, enabling us, as His children, to replenish ourselves through our worship to Him. The presence of God fills us with a depth of spiritual wisdom that provides clarity to our natural circumstances, leading to positive resolutions. This positivity serves as a catalyst for testimonies about God's goodness, which in turn brings glory to God. These testimonies affirm the life-changing effects of faith and inspire others to anchor their relationship with God. Ultimately, this leads to the upliftment of the faith community and the advancement of God's kingdom.

Psalm 81 directs the children of Israel to prioritize God in their service, emphasizing the importance of offering their praise and worship solely to Him. By their obedience, they will be awarded a promise that God will fill them when they open their mouths wide. If we embrace this principle and let nothing silence us during our worship to God, what will He bestow upon us? This question causes us to reflect on the spiritual blessings and the fulfillment that come from a sincere and unrestrained worship to God. This insight suggests that by fully engaging in worship, we can expect to receive both spiritual nourishment and support in our lives, which in turn creates a cyclical effect in our worship. **Let us worship!**

WORSHIP REFLECTION

_____
_____
_____
_____
_____
_____
_____
_____
_____
_____

GLORY MOMENTS

_____
_____
_____
_____
_____
_____
_____
_____
_____
_____

Never Runs Dry

FAVORED

Psalm 5:12

Surely, Lord, you bless the righteous; you surround
them with your favor as with a shield.

Those who embrace worship as a way of life and honor God in spirit and truth receive His favor. Embracing a worship lifestyle reflects an individual who serves God by obeying His words and instructions. Those whom God welcomes into His presence are regarded as righteous. It is important to recognize that being righteous does not imply perfection, but rather consistency. This indicates that our worship should be consistent, involving encounters with God in the sacred spaces He has established in our lives, with the anticipation of communion with Him. The righteousness of believers is imputed, meaning it is granted to us through our faith and belief in Jesus Christ (1 Cor. 1:30). The act of worship among believers is a beautiful sound and sight in the presence of

God. It brings joy to the Father when He sees His children serving Him wholeheartedly, withholding nothing; this releases unprecedented favor upon our lives.

The Psalmist clearly understands the favor of God, suggesting that he has encountered the Lord's favor consistently. The term favor in this Psalm is rendered in Hebrew as "Good Pleasures," and this is evident in various aspects of our lives. The righteous not only experience God's good pleasure, but they also receive it with great joy. This joy is seen as a radiant oar for those who embrace the good pleasure of God. It inspires the body of Christ to present authentic worship from their hearts. **Let us worship!**

WORSHIP REFLECTION

_____
_____
_____
_____
_____
_____
_____
_____
_____
_____

GLORY MOMENTS

_____
_____
_____
_____
_____
_____
_____
_____
_____
_____

See the Goodness

27

SEEING YOUR IDENTITY

Genisis 1:27
So God created mankind in his own image,
in the image of God he created them;
male and female he created them

Our worship serves as a mirror for God, reflecting His glory back to Him. Many people struggle to discover their identity and purpose in life. Isaiah 43:7 tells us that those called by His name were created for His glory. For individuals to genuinely grasp their identity, it is essential to cultivate a worship life that is guided by the Holy Spirit and our willingness to surrender. Such worship enables us to see ourselves as God sees and created us to be, understanding our purpose and advancement as we journey through this life. By living a worshipful life and surrendering to the Holy Spirit, individuals can align their self-perception with God's vision for them. Having this perception allows us to walk in our true identity.

Genesis offers us a glimpse into how God considers us and the identity bestowed upon humanity. God had the power to create us in any form, just as He did with all other creations. When He created humanity, His purpose was to reflect His image. The term "image" in this Genesis verse signifies "resemblance," and since God is Spirit, we ought to reflect Him in our spirit. The essence of our true identity is rooted in the depths of our spirit, rather than being shaped by the surroundings we inhabit. When we grasp this idea, we will become aware of the depth of our purpose, which will guide us to the profound experience of presenting our worship to God. **Let us worship!**

WORSHIP REFLECTION

_____
_____
_____
_____
_____
_____
_____
_____
_____
_____

GLORY MOMENTS

_____
_____
_____
_____
_____
_____
_____
_____
_____
_____

Jesus

28

PLIABLE IN HIS HANDS

Isaiah 64:8
And yet, O LORD, you are our Father.
We are the clay, and you are the potter.
We all are formed by your hand.

Worship makes our lives adaptable to God, meaning that our submission to Him enables us to be shaped as He intended. Allowing God to mold us in every aspect of our lives shapes us in a way that empowers us to take dominion over all He has entrusted to us, using wisdom, while walking in faith that dispels fear. This process of being shaped by God not only enhances our ability to manage our responsibilities but also instills a sense of confidence rooted in faith, which helps us overcome challenges. Overall, it motivates us to pursue our goals with courage and discernment. This discernment provokes a growth that encourages us to act decisively and wisely in our endeavors, reinforcing our worship and belief that we can navigate life's obstacles with assurance and clarity. By adopting this perspective, we enhance our capacity to achieve our purpose and render significant contributions to the kingdom of God.

Isaiah informs us that as we have a surrender relationship to God, we will experience His hand that provides guidance, safety, and love. Through this surrender, we understand that God is the one who made us and not we ourselves. Psalm 100:3 tells us that God has made us, and we are the sheep of His pasture. This imagery emphasizes our dependence on God as a shepherd, highlighting that we are cared for and nurtured by Him. Recognizing ourselves as His creation fosters a deeper worship in us for His guidance and protection. As we face each circumstance that arises, our worship demonstrates our faith in God during the process of our transformation. We are grateful to God for being the One who navigates us through it all. **Let us worship!**

WORSHIP REFLECTION

_____
_____
_____
_____
_____
_____
_____
_____
_____
_____
_____

GLORY MOMENTS

_____
_____
_____
_____
_____
_____
_____
_____
_____
_____
_____

Available to You

RENEWED STRENGTH

Isaiah 40:31
*But those who wait on the LORD will
renew their strength. They will soar on
wings like eagles; they will run and not grow
weary, they will walk and not be faint.*

Have you ever walked into worship feeling weary and come out revitalized? Worship fosters a renewal that allows us to restore our spirit. The act of being replenished is essential, as it fuels our spirit and enables us to approach each day with purpose. This renewal through worship revitalizes our spirit and prepares us to confront daily challenges with a clear sense of wisdom and vigor. Through our participation in worship, we are able to become strengthened in our mind, body, and soul, which cultivates a more enlightened connection with our purpose in God. Galatians 6:9 reminds us, *"Let us not become weary in doing good, for at the proper time we will reap a harvest if we do not give up."* Daily worship to God prevents weariness and develops a stamina that enables us to move forward with a positive outlook on our life journey.

Isaiah 40:31 inspires us to be patient and trust in the Lord. The Hebrew word for "wait" signifies a binding together, which is precisely what occurs in worship. In worship, we unite with God, as Jesus requested of the Father in John 17:21. *"I pray that they will all be one, just as you and I are one: you are in me, Father, and I am in you, and may they dwell within us, so that the world may come to believe that you sent me."* In moments of worship, we rise above all that seeks to burden us, allowing God's glory to shine through us fully. Such devotion allows us to be the example to others, allowing the Holy Spirit to continue His work in our lives. **Let us worship!**

WORSHIP REFLECTION

_____
_____
_____
_____
_____
_____
_____
_____
_____

GLORY MOMENTS

_____
_____
_____
_____
_____
_____
_____
_____
_____

Deep Places

ANCHORED JOY

Romans 15:13
*May the God of hope fill you with all joy and
peace as you trust in him, so that you may overflow
with hope by the power of the Holy Spirit.*

A joy arises from worship that anchors our spirit in the Lord and provides us with the strength to stand, as stated in Nehemiah 8:10. Through worship, we come to trust in God and encounter His peace that surpasses all understanding. Philippians 4:7. This peace allows us to concentrate on what truly matters in life and to act with discernment as we make decisions. Choosing a lifestyle of worship provides us a sense of fullness that feeds our spirits and makes our faith stronger. As we fully engage in this practice, we continue to grow spiritually and can see God in every part of our lives. Having joy when we approach God in worship also brings us into His presence expeditiously, allowing us to feel the richness of God's love and acceptance. It is important to understand this so that when we find ourselves in battle, we remain open to the Holy Spirit, who reminds us that we are overcomers and victorious.

Romans 15:13 reminds us that it is God who fills us; this pouring occurs as we surrender to God in our worship. Only those who are in a worship relationship with God can contain the overflow of His powerful presence. This overflowing hope enables us to endure our struggles, support those around us, and glorify God simultaneously. What I learned is that those who can remain positive in the midst of despair do so not because of the strength they have, but because of the deep worship they engage in with God. As mentioned, we must understand that worship is not just the songs being sung; it is the life we live before and with God. **Let us worship!**

WORSHIP REFLECTION

_____
_____
_____
_____
_____
_____
_____
_____
_____
_____

GLORY MOMENTS

_____
_____
_____
_____
_____
_____
_____
_____
_____
_____

Be Glorified

READY

Psalm 122:1
*I was glad when they said to me, "Let us
go into the house of the LORD."*

As my dear friend Pastor Jackie Copeland would say, "We are responsible for our worship." This means that we initiate and prepare ourselves to actively participate in worship to God. The Bible shows that the patriarchal fathers of the faith were prepared to worship God. They prepared everything necessary to offer an acceptable worship to God. When we enter worship, it is important that we bring all of ourselves to God with the right attitude. We see in Matthew 25:13 that Jesus tells the parable about the 10 virgins, five wise and five foolish, who were invited to the wedding feast. Essentially, the lack of preparation prevented the five foolish virgins from attending the wedding feast. How many opportunities did we miss out on because of not being prepared?

Readying our hearts to meet with God is an act of worship, attuning our ears to listen for His call. This process also positions us to receive the Lord's instructions, which brings clarity to our lives and enables the Holy Spirit to impart His gifts to us. In worship, the Holy Spirit bestows gifts that inspire us to pursue the purposes for which we were created, ultimately bringing glory to God. As we persist in living a life dedicated to God, we encounter His presence more fully, allowing us to develop spiritually and achieve our ultimate goal, also encouraging others to prepare for their worship lifestyles with God. **Let us worship!**

WORSHIP REFLECTION

_____
_____
_____
_____
_____
_____
_____
_____
_____
_____
_____

GLORY MOMENTS

_____
_____
_____
_____
_____
_____
_____
_____
_____
_____
_____

New Thing Coming

Let Us Worship!

Here is the Power of Worship Spotify Playlist.

Power Of Worship Songs